Secrets

Space keeps its secrets
                    hidden.
It does not tell.
                    Are black holes time machines?
                    Where do lost comets go?

                    Is Pluto moon or planet?

How many, how vast
        unknown galaxies beyond us?

            Do other creatures
            dwell   on distant spheres?

                        Will we ever know?

Space is silent.
It seldom answers.

        But we ask.

Myra Cohn Livingston

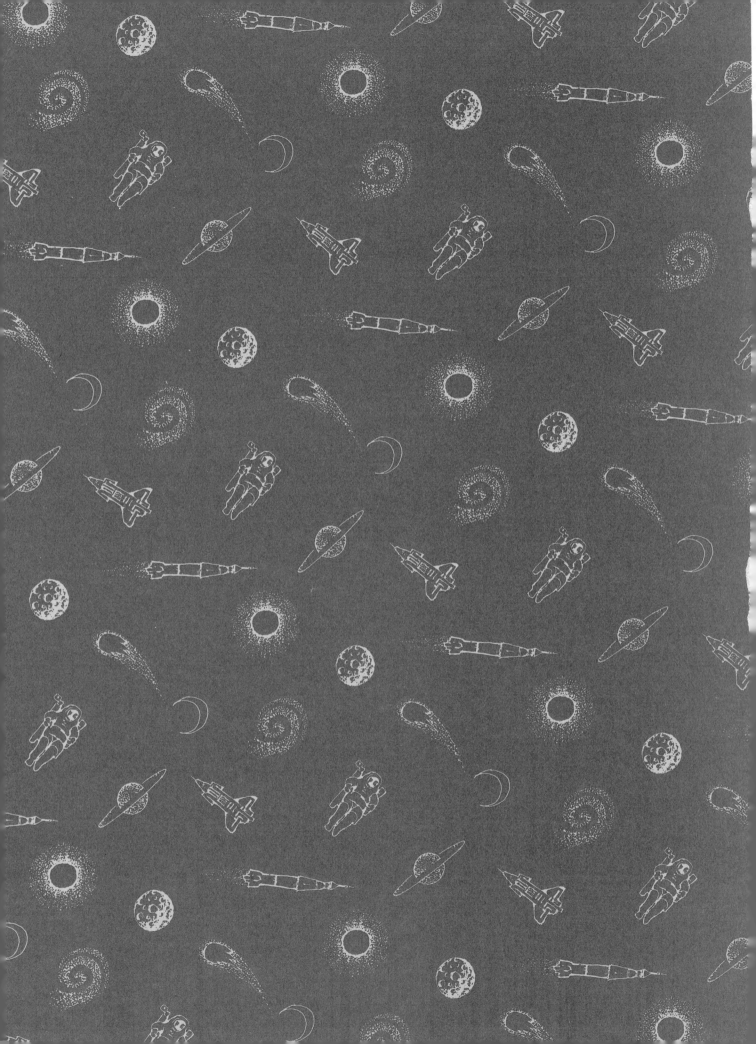

Little People™ Big Book

About
SPACE

TIME
LIFE *for*
Children™

ALEXANDRIA, VIRGINIA

Table of Contents

What's Up There?

Rocket to the Moon

Our Solar System

All Aboard for Outer Space

What's Up There?

Farther Than Far

I look into the sky and see
The leafy branches of a tree,
And higher still a bird in flight,
And higher still a cloud of white.
Beyond the cloud is lots more sky,
Farther than far, higher than high.
And where it ends, another place
Is filled with space and space and space.

Margaret Hillert

Beyond the Milky Way
by Cecile Schoberle

Out of my window,
  I can see between the buildings.
Between the buildings, I can see
  the twilight blue of the summer sky.

In the sky, I can see the lights from
  an airplane blinking . . . off . . . and on.
Past the airplane, I can see
  the misty clouds floating by.

Above the clouds, I can see diamond-bright
stars and the swirling Milky Way.

Beyond the Milky Way, I can imagine
the glowing planets.

 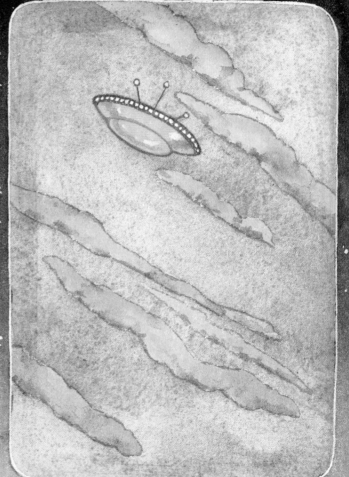

On a planet,
I wonder if there's someone else
    who can see between her buildings.
Between the buildings, maybe she can see
    the velvet blue of her summer sky.

In the sky, perhaps she can see the
    spaceship lights flashing . . . off . . .
    and on.
Past the spaceship, maybe she can see
    the feathery clouds drifting by.

Above the clouds, maybe she can see
the crystal-clear stars and the flowing
Milky Way.

Beyond the Milky Way, perhaps she can see
the twirling planet, Earth.
And does she wonder if I am here on Earth,
looking out my window?

9

DON'T FALL OFF!

Today we know the earth is round. But for many, many years, people said, "The earth can't be round. If it were, people on the other side of the Earth would be walking upside down—or they would fall off!" No wonder people from long ago came up with so many unusual ideas about the shape the world is in!

Some early people thought the Earth went on and on. It was one big flat piece of land that never ended. But people wondered how the sun could go down on one side and come up on the other side every morning. They decided that somebody put the sun into a boat every night and rowed it back across the world!

Long ago in India people believed the Earth was shaped like half a circle with a flat top. It was resting on the backs of some great big elephants. Why didn't the elephants fall down? They were standing on the back of a giant turtle! Why didn't the turtle fall down? It was swimming in a great big ocean!

Some people who lived in the time called the Middle Ages thought the Earth was a big pancake floating in a giant pool of water (not maple syrup!).

The maps from this time show a ring of water around the Earth. Wild and unusual things are shown living in far-off lands at the edge of the world. There are pictures of monster fish, people with the heads of dogs, and giants in caves. It was believed that when ships came to the end of the water, they would fall off.

Many old stories say the world was shaped like a giant woman. Her hair was the grass and trees. Her eyes became the sun and moon.

As time went on ideas began to change. People sailed around the world. They learned about the real shape of the Earth. And finally, when the first astronauts went into space, they saw it for themselves. The Earth is round.

DID YOU EVER WONDER
ABOUT SPACE

Why is the sun so bright?
The sun is a star, just like the stars you see at night. Stars are made of hot gases that radiate energy, like heat and light. Most stars are so far away from the Earth that their light looks very dim to us. But the sun is much closer to us than the other stars. That's why it seems so bright.

Where does the sun go at night?
Nowhere! The sun just looks as if it's going away. That's because the Earth is always moving. It spins like a top. When one side of the Earth faces the sun, the other side is in darkness. It's daytime on the sunny side and nighttime on the dark side.

12

Why do stars twinkle?

Stars twinkle because their light beams pass through Earth's atmosphere. The light is bent by the layers and pockets of air, which are all different temperatures. But when astronauts are out in space looking at stars, the stars don't twinkle.

What is a shooting star?

A shooting star isn't really a star at all. It's a meteor. Meteors are pieces of space rock or metal. A meteor gets very, very hot when it flies through Earth's air. It gets so hot, it glows. It usually burns up in a flash before it gets to Earth. But some meteors are so big, they don't burn up. They crash into Earth. But this is extremely rare. You don't have to worry about being hit by a meteor!

13

How far away are the moon and the stars?

The moon is 240 thousand miles from the Earth. That seems far away, but the moon is actually closer to Earth than anything else in space! It is much closer than the stars. A spaceship takes only a few days to fly to the moon. But it would take thousands of years to fly to the nearest star! The stars are trillions of miles away.

Will we ever live on the moon?

Right now, people can't live on the moon. The moon has no air for us to breathe or water for us to drink. No plants or animals can live there either.

When the astronauts went to the moon they took their own supplies of air, water, and food with them. That is the only way for people to survive on the moon. Maybe someday we will be able to build a giant space station on the moon. It will be an indoor city, like a shopping mall, with everything we need to live inside. If you lived in the space station, you would be a moon pioneer!

Do space creatures exist?

No one has ever seen a creature from space. But there may be space creatures living somewhere. There are millions of stars. Some of them may have planets like Earth orbiting around them. Scientists think that space creatures may live on some of these planets. In fact, scientists send radio signals far, far out into space to let other space creatures know we're here. They hope someday someone will send a message back to us.

15

Lifting the Sky
A Native American Legend about the Big Dipper

Have you ever looked at the Big Dipper? The Big Dipper is a constellation, a group of seven stars that form a picture. If the seven stars are connected they look like a big spoon. Hundreds of years ago, people looked at the stars and saw all kinds of pictures. And they made up wonderful stories to explain these star pictures. Here is a Native American story about the constellation we call The Big Dipper.

his story happened a long time ago, a very long time ago when the world was just made. Then the sky was so low that tall people bumped their heads against it. People had to walk bent over, which was very uncomfortable.

Finally, the wise men from all the different Indian tribes held a meeting to see what they could do about lifting the sky.

"We can lift the sky," said the wise men of the council, "if we all push at the same time. We will need the help of all the animals and all the people and all the birds."

"How will we know when to push?" asked another of the wise men. "We don't talk the same language. How can we get everyone to push at the same time?"

That puzzled the men of the council. At last, one of the wise men said, "We can use a signal. When the time comes to push, someone can yell 'Ya Ho!', and we will all push together."

Finally the day came for lifting the sky. The people all brought poles with them to push against the sky. They made their poles from giant fir trees. The birds picked up the cut branches. Bears, wolves, rabbits, and even the coyotes came out of the forest and raised their poles to touch the sky.

Now on that day in another part of the forest, three young men went out to hunt.

Their village had no meat, and the people were hungry. Soon the hunters sighted tracks of a band of elk and began to follow them.

The hunters were skilled. Their quivers were filled with feathered arrows with tips of flint. One hunter had brought his best hunting dog. But the elk were wise and swift. They managed to stay just out of range. The hunters kept following the elk. The hunters were so determined to catch them that they didn't notice that the elk were leading them deeper and deeper into the forest.

Soon the hunters found themselves at the very end of the forest—at the place where the Sky World meets the Earth.

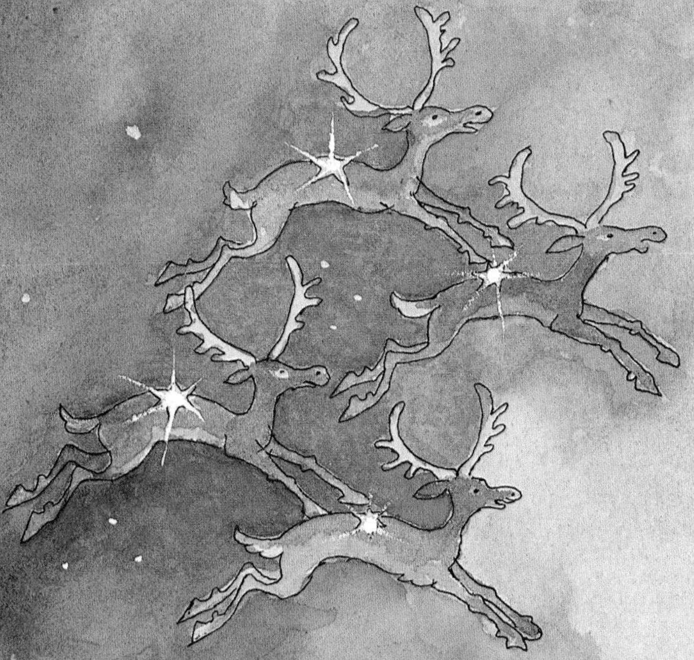

At that moment, on the other side of the forest, the wise man said the words that would lift the sky.

"Ya Ho!"

Everyone who heard the signal pushed. Sure enough, the sky moved up a little bit. The hunters who were still tracking the elk didn't notice.

"Ya Ho!" shouted the wise man a second time. This time everyone dug their heels into the ground and pushed with all their strength. The sky moved up a few inches more.

At that moment, four of the elk jumped right into the Sky World. Of course the hunters jumped right after them.

19

Everyone below kept on shouting and lifting until they raised the sky right to where it is today. And they also lifted the hunters, the dog, and the four elk—right into the Sky World.

In the Sky World, they were changed into stars. And at night you can still see them. The four elk form the bowl of the Big Dipper. The three hunters make up the handle. And if you look really carefully, you can see a little star next to the middle hunter. That's his faithful dog. And that's where they will be forever —the three hunters and the dog, as always, tracking and following the elk across the night sky.

Rocket to the Moon

Naughty Little Brown Mouse

Naughty little brown mouse,
whiskers on his face,
stowed aboard a rocket
bound for outer space,
they lifted off from Houston
on Tuesday afternoon,
the mouse ate cheese that Sunday
in the mountains of the moon.

Jack Prelutsky

23

Footprints on the Moon
by Megan Stine

For many years, people wondered about space. What would it be like to visit another world? What would it be like to walk on the moon?

Three astronauts were going to find out. Neil Armstrong, Buzz Aldrin, and Michael Collins sat in a tiny spaceship. Soon they were going to the moon!

But no one had ever done it before. No one had ever seen the moon up close.

What would it be like? Could a man or woman breathe on the moon? Could a spaceship land there?

Was the ground solid or was it soft and squishy?

Since no one had ever been to the moon, no one knew the answers!

Some scientists worried that the surface of the moon was really a deep layer of dust—as deep as a pool or a lake. They thought the astronauts and their spaceship might sink into the dust and disappear!

So, many months before, several spaceships had been sent to visit the moon *without* people on board. The spaceships took pictures of the moon and found out what the moon was like. Then scientists and astronauts planned the moon landing.

On July 16, 1969, a rocket was ready. It was very tall, as tall as a building with 30 floors. On top of the rocket was a much smaller space-craft. It had two sections, hooked together. One section, the *lunar excursion module*, was the part that would land on the moon. The other, the *command module*, was smaller than a car. That's where the three astronauts were waiting to blast off.

Their hearts were pounding as the countdown began. 10–9–8–7–6 seconds to go. 5–4–3–2–1—blast off!

The Apollo 11 mission was on its way!

As the powerful rocket lifted into the sky, the astronauts felt strange. Their bodies were pressed against their seats. For a few minutes, it felt as if three or four people were lying on top of them.

But the astronauts knew what to do. And they knew that the heavy feeling would be over soon. How did they know? They had been training

for this moon flight for several years.

After blast-off, the rocket fell away and the two smaller sections went zooming through space. The astronauts looked out the window. What do you think they saw? Nothing but darkness. Outer space was completely black.

Inside, the spaceship was very cramped. The astronauts could barely move. They had plain, cold food to eat. They drank liquids from a tube. They couldn't stand up or walk around.

The trip to the moon took four days.

Can you imagine spending four days inside your car?

Finally the spacecraft neared the moon. Now it was time for the ship to split into two sections. One section, the command module, would circle around the moon the whole time.

The other section—the lunar excursion module (LEM)—would land on the moon. The crew called the LEM the *Eagle*.

Someone had to stay inside the command module. The other two astronauts would walk on the moon. Neil Armstrong and Buzz Aldrin were the astronauts who had been chosen to land on the moon. Michael Collins knew he would have to stay in the command module. He would have the important job of making sure they all got back to Earth safely.

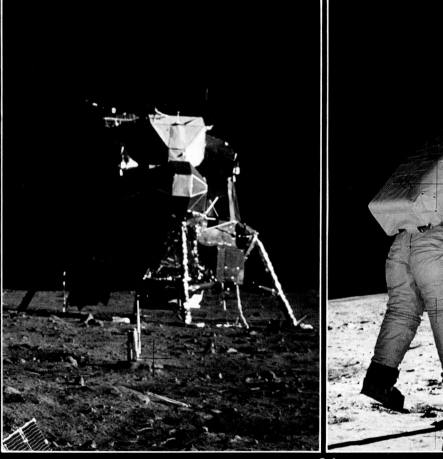

they land? A landing spot had already been chosen for them. But when the astronauts got close, they saw that it was filled with boulders. If they landed there, they might crash!

Quickly Neil Armstrong took the controls. He guided the *Eagle* to a safer, smoother spot.

Millions of people on Earth were watching the moon landing on television. Everyone wanted to see the first man on the moon.

Soon Neil Armstrong put on the special space suit he had to wear on the moon. Then he climbed out of the *Eagle*. He started to climb down a ladder to the moon's surface. He pulled a cord to turn on a television camera.

Everyone on Earth waited to hear what he would say.

"That's one small step for man— one giant leap for mankind," Neil Armstrong said as he jumped off the bottom step.

A few minutes later, Buzz Aldrin joined Neil Armstrong. Together they began to explore this strange, new world. To Neil, the bare gray moon had a beauty all its own.

As the two astronauts walked, their boots left big, deep footprints. Guess what? The surface of the moon was dusty! There was a fine,

27

powdery dust everywhere. The astronauts noticed that their footprints didn't change or blow away. And they knew why. It was because there was no wind or rain on the moon. In fact, their footprints will probably never change. They are still there today!

For two hours and 14 minutes, the astronauts worked on the moon. They collected samples of moon rocks and moon dust. They took photographs. They placed some scientific equipment and experiments on the moon. The two astronauts even set up an American flag.

The work was hard. And the moon was a strange place. It was burning hot in the daytime—too hot for human beings to live there. At night, it was terribly cold. There was no air to breathe.

But the astronauts had space suits to protect them. Inside the bulky suits, there was an air supply. There were also many tubes of water to keep the astronauts cool. Without their space suits, the astronauts would not have been able to stand the heat. They would have died.

When the two hours were up, Neil Armstrong did not want to leave the surface of the moon. He wanted to explore some more, to collect more moon rocks. And he wanted to spend a little more time on the beautiful moon. Being on the moon was exciting and fun!

But Neil and Buzz knew that they had to follow orders. Many danger-

ous moments in the spaceflight were still ahead. The most dangerous moment would come the next day. That's when the *Eagle* had to connect with the command module again. Would they make it?

Neil and Buzz climbed back into the *Eagle* to get some sleep. The next morning, it was time to leave. They fired the burners and blasted off from the moon.

Goodbye, moon!

A short while later, the *Eagle* hooked up with the command module. Michael Collins, the third astronaut, was so glad to see his friends! He was happy that they were safe. Now they could go home together.

The astronauts had done something that no one had done before. They had gone to the moon, and walked there, and left human footprints behind.

Now, as they headed home, they looked up into a pitch-black sky. And what do you think they saw? They saw the Earth, glowing like a huge, beautiful moon in the sky. No one had ever seen the Earth from so far away before. The astronauts took pictures. Now everyone knows how the Earth looks from outer space.

MOON RIDDLES

The moon is full tonight—full of laughs and giggles.

Why did the moon ask Mars to move over?
It was taking up space!

What holds up the moon?
Moonbeams!

What day of the week does the moon like?
Moonday!

Who was the first person in space?
The man in the moon!

When was the Milky Way created?
When the cow jumped over the moon!

Why are the moon and a cow alike?
They both contain a moo!

Why didn't the moon finish its lunch?
It was full!

The Moon's My Balloon
by H.L. Ross

Benny Bunny went to his best friend's birthday party. There was a triple-layered carrot cake and carrot ice cream and all sorts of fun games and prizes. But best of all, as he was walking out the door to go home, he got his very own balloon.

It was a wonderful balloon. It was big and round and bouncy and yellow and it bobbed in the air above his head at the end of a long string.

As he walked home between his mother and his father he couldn't take his eyes off that wonderful yellow balloon.

"Make sure you hold on to the string," said his father.

"You wouldn't want to lose that balloon," said his mother.

"Don't worry, I'll hold on tight," said Benny.

But just then, the wind picked up and tugged at the balloon, as if to say, *Give me that balloon. I want it. It's mine!*

"Oh, no, it's not! It's mine!" said Benny. But the wind was stronger than he was and it plucked the balloon right out of his furry little paws.

"My balloon!" he cried as it floated

up beyond his reach and stuck in the branches of an apple tree.

"Don't worry, I'll get it," his father said. Quickly, he climbed the apple tree. But just as he got to the end of the branch the wind came along again and took the balloon still further away. Up, up, up, higher and higher into the clouds until it was the tiniest yellow speck high in the sky. Then it disappeared altogether.

Benny cried and cried.

He hardly touched his supper that night. His mother and father shook their heads sadly, but what could they do?

That night, as Benny was getting ready for bed, he looked out the window. His little bunny heart began to pound. What was that floating up in the sky? It was big and round and bouncy and yellow!

"Look, Mother!" he cried.

She came over to the window and looked out.

"See, Mother?" said Benny. "It's come back! My—"

"Moon!" said his mother, finishing for him. "And a very full moon it is tonight."

"But —" Benny began, but his mother hustled him off to bed with a kiss and a hug. It had been a long and busy day.

Benny snuggled down beneath the covers and closed his eyes.

It was still nighttime when he awoke. He went to the window and looked out. There, floating right over his house, bigger and brighter and more beautiful than ever, was his big yellow balloon. The string hung down and dangled just a few feet above the grass of his own front lawn. If he hurried down there, maybe he could grab it before the wind came along and took his balloon away again!

35

Benny ran downstairs and out onto the lawn. Standing on his tippy-toes, he just reached the string. He gave it a good tug. But what was this? The string was tugging back! Before Benny knew it, his little feet had left the grass and he was floating up, up, up, higher and higher into the starry night, holding tight to the string of his yellow balloon.

Benny looked down. He saw his house and his yard and the pathway to his friend's house and the apple tree. He saw woods and streams and a fox slinking across silver meadows. An owl making his nightly rounds flapped past him.

"Who-ooo-ooo are you?" he asked.

"I'm Benny," said Benny, "and this is my balloon."

"That's no balloon," said the owl. "That's the moon!"

"Then the moon's my balloon!" Benny called after the owl.

36

All night long, he bobbed gently along in a sea of twinkling stars. Just as dawn was breaking, he floated back down to earth, back to his own lawn. And Benny knew it was time to let go of the string.

The next thing he knew, someone was shaking him.

"Wake up, Benny!" said his father.

"Why do you have your arm sticking up in the air like that?" his mother wanted to know.

"Oh!" said Benny. "I guess I just didn't want to let go of my balloon!"

"Right after breakfast," said his father, "we're taking you to the store to buy a new one."

"That's okay," said Benny with a smile. "I don't need a new one."

"You don't?" both his parents asked at once.

"The moon's my balloon," said Benny. "The most beautiful balloon there is!"

Our Solar System

Valentine for Earth

Oh, it will be fine
To rocket through space
And see the reverse
Of the moon's dark face,

To travel to Saturn
Or Venus or Mars,
Or maybe discover
Some uncharted stars.

But do they have anything
Better than we?
Do you think, for instance,
They have a blue sea
For sailing and swimming?
Do planets have hills
With raspberry thickets
Where a song sparrow fills

The summer with music?
And do they have snow
To silver the roads
Where the school buses go?

Oh, I'm all for rockets
And worlds cold or hot,
But I'm wild in love
With the planet we've got!

Frances Frost

A Tour of the Solar System

What would it be like to travel through space and see the planets in our solar system up close? So far, only telescopes on Earth or spacecraft with no one on board have given us pictures of the planets. Someday, you may have a chance to board a spaceship for Mars or Jupiter. But for now, come along on this picture tour of our space neighbors—the planets in our solar system.

The Sun's Family

Our Earth is one of nine planets that travel around the sun. The planets look like nine big balls as they move slowly in egg-shaped circles or orbits. Mercury is closest to the sun. Then come Venus, Earth, Mars, Jupiter, Saturn, Uranus, Neptune, and Pluto.

The sun is a huge star that gives off its own light and heat. The planets reflect the sun's light. Instead of twinkling like stars, they usually shine with a steady light. We call the sun and its nine planets our solar system.

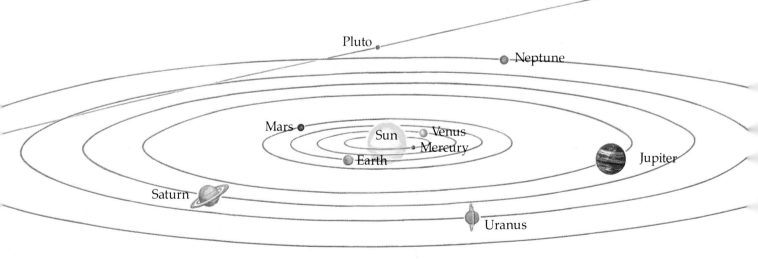

A Planet the Size of Our Moon

Mercury is a small planet, not much bigger than our moon. It looks like our moon, too. It has no rivers or oceans, just a dry, stony desert with big craters and small mountains. Scientists believe that long ago Mercury's rocky surface was very soft. Large rocks and other objects flying through space crashed into Mercury. They left holes, or craters, in the soft crust.

The Twin Planets

Venus is Earth's closest neighbor. It's about the same size as Earth. Venus and Earth are often called the Twin Planets.

Venus is the hottest planet in the solar system. Thick clouds of poisonous gases surround Venus. They are like a blanket that traps in the heat. The temperature can get as high as 900 degrees F.

This is the third planet from the Sun — the Earth. Sometimes the Earth is called the Big Blue Marble. Can you see why? The white swirls you see are the clouds. The brown and green are land. And the blue is water. As you can see, the Earth is mostly water. Earth is our planet, the only place in the solar system with the perfect conditions for human life.

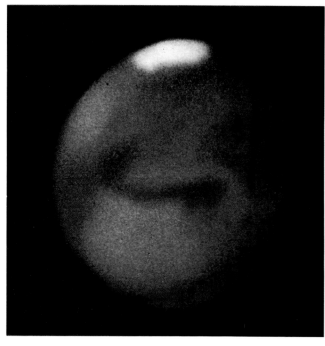

The Red Planet

This is what Mars looks like through a telescope. People used to think there might be life on Mars. They thought the long black lines in this picture looked like canals. If Mars had canals, they thought, the canals might have been built by living beings. Many years later a spacecraft flew by Mars. It sent back pictures showing that the dark lines on Mars were not canals. They were empty river beds. Because of space probes we now know that Mars is a cold, dry desert world. Ice caps at the north and south poles probably hold the only water left on Mars.

The picture below shows the Viking Lander on Mars. Can you see why Mars is called the Red Planet? It is covered with rusty-red rocks and dust. Terrible winds whip up tornado-like storms of swirling dust, so that the sky above Mars looks pinkish brown.

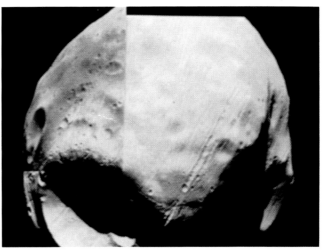

Is this a bumpy potato? Actually, it is one of the moons of Mars. Mars has two tiny moons — Deimos and Phobos — that circle around it, just as our moon orbits the Earth. Wouldn't it be strange to look up at night and see two moons in the sky?

The Giant Planets

Jupiter is the giant of the nine planets. It is so big that all the other planets could fit inside it. Somebody once figured out that a person riding a bicycle nonstop would take five years to pedal around the center of Jupiter. But the rider would have a big problem. Jupiter does not have a hard surface! It is made up of liquids and gases with only a small rocky core at the center.

There is a Giant Red Spot on Jupiter where scientists think a wild hurricane has been raging for hundreds of years. Below is a close-up picture of it. Can you find it in the big picture of Jupiter?

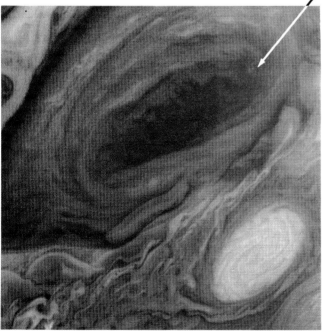

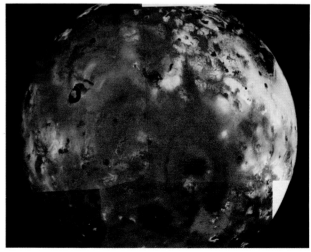

This is a picture of Io, one of Jupiter's 16 moons. It is covered with volcanoes. Some people say the surface of this moon looks like a pizza. What do you think?

44

Can you guess the name of this planet? It is Saturn. Saturn is another giant planet, though not as big as Jupiter. Like Jupiter, Saturn doesn't have a hard surface. The gases and liquids that swirl around it are made of chemicals that are lighter than water. Saturn would float if you could find an ocean big enough to hold it! Scientists keep finding more moons around Saturn. So far, they have discovered 21!

Saturn is one of the most beautiful planets in our solar system. This is a close-up picture of some of the dazzling rings that orbit around it. These rings are not as solid as they look. They are made of pieces of ice and rock, some as small as pebbles, others as big as boulders.

The Distant Cousins

Uranus is another planet that is made of gas and liquid. Uranus rolls around the sun on its side. This peculiar way of traveling gives it the longest summers and winters in the solar system — about 21 years. Uranus has 15 moons and 12 rings. The rings are very dark and hard to see.

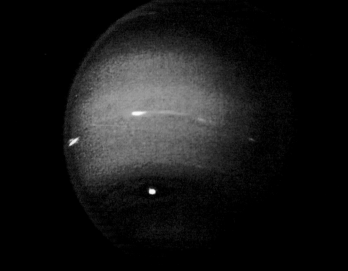

This is Neptune. It has 8 moons. From the photographs sent back by a space probe, scientists learned that Neptune has a huge dark spot that covers an area equal to the whole surface of the Earth.

Neptune has three rings, but they are so dark that they don't always show up in photographs.

The Smallest Planet

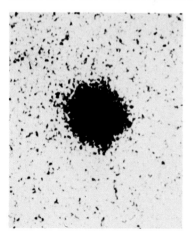

The ninth and smallest planet is Pluto. It is so far away that it is almost impossible to see — even with a telescope. The black spot in this photograph is the best picture we have of Pluto. Pluto is made of rock and has one tiny moon that circles it. Some scientists think that Pluto itself might have been a moon once. Perhaps it circled around Neptune or some other planet and was bumped out of its orbit long ago. Pluto takes 247 Earth years to go around the sun. For 20 years of its orbit, it passes inside Neptune's orbit. During that period, Neptune becomes the planet farthest from the sun.

Beyond the Solar System

Are there any other planets that have not yet been found? Many scientists believe that there may be another solar system circling around another star among the billions of stars in space. Perhaps one of our space probes will find it someday!

All Aboard for Outer Space

Space Swing

When my swing goes up to the sky of blue,
I can touch the sun with the tip of my shoe.
Away up high where the white clouds race,
I play I'm an astronaut out in space.
I guess that a moon trip might be fun,
But here in my swing I can touch the sun.

Margaret Hillert

ROCKETS! ROCKETS!

Wouldn't it be fun to blast off in a rocket all your own?
Play this game and you can pretend you are taking off for
outer space.

Rockets! Rockets! All in a row.
Rockets! Rockets! Ready to go!
Listen, the engine is starting to fire
Blast off! We're going higher and
HIGHER!

Rockets! Rockets! All in a row.   Rockets! Rockets! Ready to go!

Put your hands together in   *Lift your hands until*
front of you like this.   *they're above your head.*

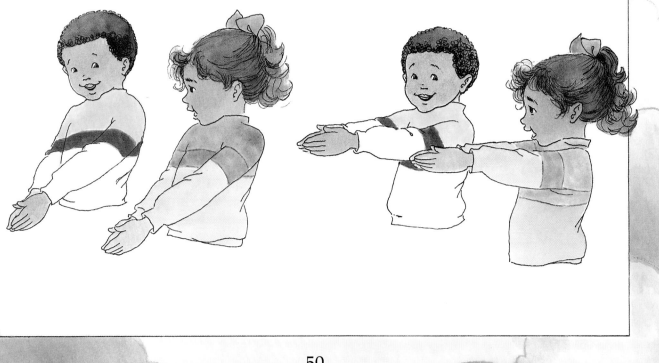

Listen, the engine is starting to fire

Clap your hands together when you say "Fire."

Blast off!

Open your hands out to the sides above your head.

We're going higher and

HIGHER!

Jump!

All About Space Travel
by Sally Ride

Sally Ride was the first American woman to go into space. She was an astronaut on two space shuttle missions. The space shuttle is the world's first spaceplane. It blasts off into space without the help of big booster rockets. Then it flies around the Earth for several days or a week. Then it lands on Earth just like an airplane.

What's it like to be an astronaut? Is it hard work? Is it fun? How do you eat and sleep? Lots of children have asked Sally Ride those questions. Here are some of her answers—in her own words.

52

The best part of being in space is being weightless. It feels wonderful to be able to float without effort: to slither up, down, and around the inside of the shuttle just like a seal; to be upside down as often as I'm right side up and have it make no difference. On Earth being upside down feels different because gravity is pulling the blood toward my head. In space I feel exactly the same whether my head is toward the floor or toward the ceiling.

When I'm weightless, some things don't change. My heart beats at about the same rate as it does on Earth. I can still swallow and digest food.

I *look* a little different, though—all astronauts do. Since the fluid in our bodies is not pulled toward our feet as it is on Earth, more of this fluid stays in our faces and upper bodies. This makes our faces a little fatter and gives us puffy-looking cheeks. We are also about an inch taller while in orbit because in weightlessness our spines are not compressed.

During my first day in space, I had to learn how to move around. I started out trying to "swim" through the air, but that didn't work at all. Before long I discovered that I had to push off from one of the walls if I wanted to get across the room. At first I would push off a little too hard and crash into the opposite wall, but I soon learned to wind my way around with very gentle pushes.

Sally floats on the flight deck. Do you see her flying calculators?

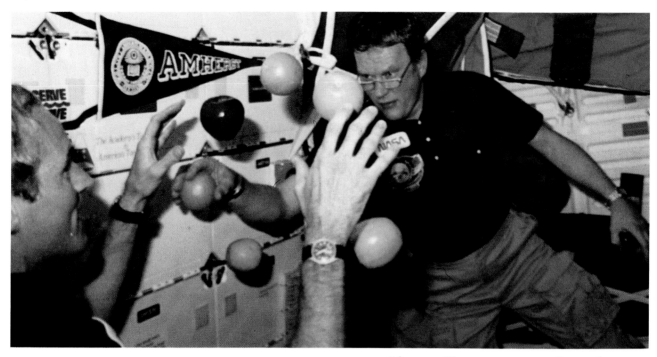

Above: *Two astronauts have fun juggling their lunch!*

We gather on the mid-deck to enjoy meals together like a family. But we don't look like a family sitting down to lunch on Earth. We don't eat at a table; our tables are the trays strapped to our legs. We don't sit in chairs. Each of us finds a comfortable spot—maybe floating near the ceiling, or upside down in the middle of the cabin.

We each have a knife and fork, but our most useful pieces of silverware are spoons and scissors. We need scissors to snip open the foil pouches of hot dogs, the packages of peanuts, and the plastic cartons of macaroni. Then we use the spoons to get the food to our mouths. Most of our food is deliberately made sticky enough to stay on a spoon and not float away as we try to eat it. In fact,

we can flip our spoons all the way across the cabin and the food won't come off—usually! Sometimes a blob of pudding escapes from a spinning spoon, and we have to catch it before it splatters on a wall.

Astronauts can't always resist the fun of playing with weightless food. On one of my flights, we set a cookie floating in the middle of the room and then "flew" an astronaut, with his mouth wide open, across the cabin to capture it. We race to capture spinning carrots and bananas and practice catching spoonfuls of food in our mouths while they twirl in mid-air. These tricks are easy in space, but I don't recommend trying them on Earth.

It is surprisingly easy to get comfortable and fall asleep in space. Every astronaut sleeps differently. Some sleep upside down, some sideways, some right side up. Some crawl into their sleeping bags and then tie them to anything handy, to keep them floating in one place. Others use the thin bags alone as blankets and wedge themselves into corners. Still others simply float in the middle of the cabin, sometimes cushioning their heads in case they drift gently against the ceiling—or another sleeping astronaut.

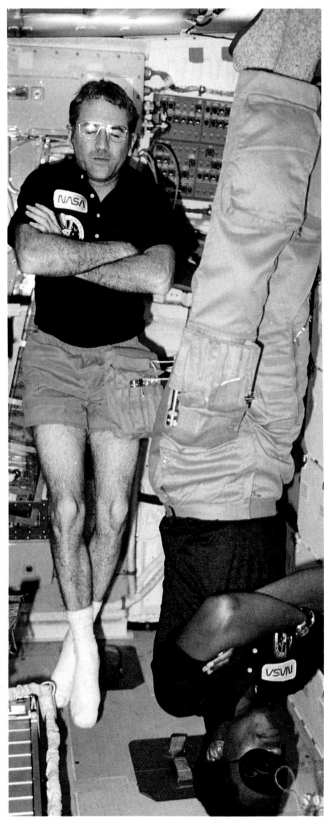

In space, you can sleep upside down if you want to!

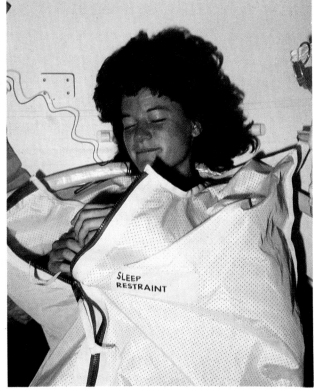

Sweet dreams, Sally!

Right: *Bruce McCandless, an astronaut on another shuttle mission, floats in space using a jetpack.*

Most of our work can be done inside the space shuttle, but sometimes we have to go outside, either to make repairs or to perform an experiment. While we are inside, we are protected from the emptiness of outer space, but outside there is no air to breathe, and the temperature can be very hot or very cold. To leave the protection of the space shuttle, we have to put on spacesuits.

Floating out into space, the space-walking astronauts become human satellites. *They* are orbiting Earth! Their view stretches from horizon to horizon and across the whole sky.

Doug's New Address: Space Colony One

by Cathy East Dubowski and Mark Dubowski

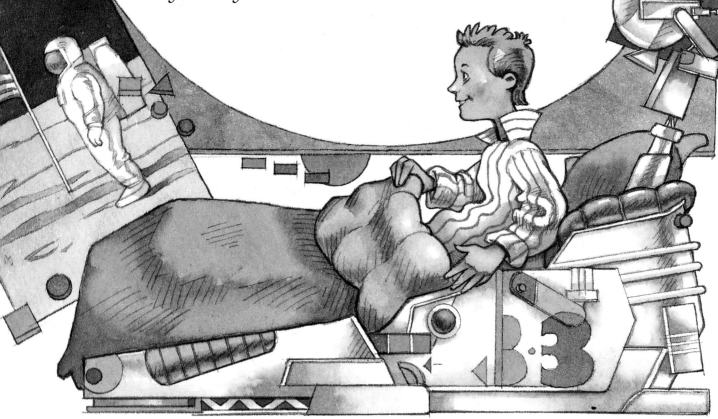

oug woke up, and for a moment he thought he was still back on Earth— in his own bed, in his own house, in the town where he'd grown up.

But he wasn't on Earth. He was in space—thousands of miles above the planet. His family had just moved to Space Colony One. Over 10,000 people worked and lived here. They came from nearly every country on Earth.

Doug's dad had a new job running a factory where high-speed robots made computers. His mom was going to study the planets using Space Colony One's superpowered telescopes.

"Think how exciting it will be to live in space!" Doug's dad had said before the move. "We'll be pioneers!"

Doug's dream was to be a space explorer. On the wall of his new room was a poster of Neil Armstrong, the first person on the moon. "Maybe one day kids will hang up a poster about me!" thought Doug.

"Doug Drysdale, first guy on Mars!"

Doug heard a tapping on his window. He pushed a button to slide open a window screen. Out on the deck a freckle-faced girl pressed her nose to the glass. It was Astrid, who lived in the apartment next door.

"Wake up, Earthling!" she shouted. "You're going to be late for your first day at school!"

"Meet you at the front door, Space Girl," said Doug. Astrid laughed. Her parents were from Earth, but she had never been there. She was one of the first kids born in space, and she had spent her whole life on Space Colony One.

Astrid had a paper route. Every morning she delivered *The Daily Orbit* on her way to school. Today she was taking Doug with her to show him the neighborhood.

Doug pulled on his jeans, his sneakers, and his lucky baseball jersey and ran downstairs. His mom and dad were at the kitchen table.

RB-7, his family's personal robot, was making breakfast at the microwave oven. "How about some breakfast, Douglas?" said the robot. "I'm making Soybean Surprise."

"I think I'll just have a Vitamin Shake this morning, Robby," Doug said, using RB-7's nickname. He drank it on the way out the door.

Outside, Astrid was waiting on an electric scooter loaded with papers. "Hop on!" she called.

"This is awesome!" said Doug.

"Every morning on the way to school, I drop off today's paper and pick up yesterday's to be recycled," said Astrid. "If I didn't have this paper route, I guess my mom would make me walk or take the monorail, like everybody else."

"I noticed that!" said Doug. "Even grown-ups don't drive their own cars here!"

"They don't really need them," said Astrid. "Space Colony One is only four miles around."

To Doug, Space Colony One looked a lot like a small town on Earth, if you built it inside a big shopping mall. There were apartments, stores, movie theaters, and parks. Trees and flowers grew along the short streets. But there was no blue sky, no clouds or birds. Instead there were windows in the ceiling that looked out toward mirrors that reflected sunlight inside.

"Hey," said Doug, "what makes the weather here?"

"We do, of course," said Astrid. "The temperature—even daylight and nighttime—are all controlled by computers!"

"Then I guess the ball games never get rained out!" said Doug.

"We never have to bother with rain or snow here," said Astrid.

Doug thought about that. "What! No snowmen?" he said.

"What's a snowman?" asked Astrid.

"Never mind," said Doug. "I'll

show you some pictures sometime."

Astrid threw a fresh copy of *The Daily Orbit* onto a porch and Doug leaned down to pick up the old copy from the recycling box by the curb.

Up ahead, there were no more houses and stores.

"Even in space you need to eat your vegetables," said Astrid. "Now entering Section Two: a Space Colony farm."

But it was not like any farm Doug had ever seen. Corn, wheat, and other crops grew above them on four levels, like giant shelves built right up the sides of the space station.

"My uncle works here," said Astrid. "He's a fish farmer."

"A what farmer?" said Doug.

"Fish farmer! Since we don't have any lakes or streams, my uncle raises our fish in specially built ponds way up on top, above the fields.

"Now for my favorite part of the morning . . . the docking port," Astrid said. She drove the scooter into a big elevator. It took them up one of the spokes that connected the outer wheel of the space colony to the hub in the center. As they moved slowly toward the middle, Doug and Astrid felt themselves getting lighter and lighter.

"There's no gravity in the hub, you know," said Astrid. "In fact, there's no gravity anywhere on Space Colony One."

"I know," said Doug. "Dad showed

me when we got here that Space
Colony One is like a big wheel going
round and round."

"Right," said Astrid. "That makes
centrifugal force, and that's what
holds things down here, instead
of gravity."

"I know all about centrifugal force
from those big spinning rides at the
State Fair," said Doug.

"What's a State Fair?" asked Astrid.

"I can show you some pictures of

that too," said Doug.

By now they had reached the center where transport vehicles from Earth and other planets were bringing people and supplies to Space Colony One. It was the only place on the space station where there was no centrifugal force—and Doug, Astrid, and Astrid's scooter were completely weightless. Floating through the hub was kind of like flying . . . and kind of like swimming. "I wish my friends on Earth could see this!" Doug said.

Through a window he could see a huge round mirror floating beside Space Colony One. It reflected sunlight to the solar panels around the hub and made all the electricity for the colony.

Doug and Astrid took the elevator down to Section Five, and soon they weren't weightless anymore.

Beep-beep! Astrid looked at her watch. "It's almost time for school and I've got three more papers to deliver."

"I'll do them," said Doug. He tossed the papers—and each one landed neatly at the right doorstep.

"Hey!" said Astrid. "You're pretty good. Where'd you learn to throw like that?"

"I used to pitch in Little League baseball back home," said Doug as they glided into the schoolyard.

"Hmm," said Astrid. "Have you ever played Space Ball?"

Astrid parked the scooter and several kids ran up.

"Hey, everybody, this is Doug," Astrid said. "He's an Earthling—but don't hold it against him!"

All the kids laughed, and Doug laughed too. On Earth, Doug had only dreamed of adventure. On Space Colony One, those dreams would come true.

Little People™ Big Book About SPACE

TIME-LIFE for CHILDREN ™

Publisher: Robert H. Smith
Managing Editor: Neil Kagan
Editorial Directors: Jean Burke Crawford,
　　　　　　　　Patricia Daniels
Editorial Coordinator: Elizabeth Ward
Marketing Director: Ruth P. Stevens
Product Manager: Margaret Mooney
Production Manager: Prudence G. Harris
Administrative Assistant: Rebecca C. Christoffersen
Editorial Consultants: Jacqueline A. Ball, Sara Mark

PRODUCED BY PARACHUTE PRESS, INC.

Editorial Director: Joan Waricha
Editors: Christopher Medina, Jane Stine,
　　　Wendy Wax
Writers: Julia Andrews, Cathy East Dubowski,
　　　Mark Dubowski, Lisa Eisenberg,
　　　Walter Retan, H.L. Ross, Megan Stine,
　　　Jean Waricha
Designer: Gill Speirs
Illustrators: Shirley Beckes (p. 12-15), Pat and
　　　Robin DeWitt (p. 32-37), G. Brian
　　　Karas (p. 10-11), Barbara Lanza
　　　(p. 6-9), Allan Neuwirth (p. 30-31),
　　　Gill Speirs (endpapers), John Speirs
　　　(cover, p. 4-5, 16-21, 22-23, 38-39,
　　　48-49), Linda Weller (p. 50-51),
　　　Fred Winkowski (p. 58-63)
Photographs: Courtesy of NASA (p. 25-39, 52-57).
　　　Moon-Photo Credit: Frank Whitney/
　　　The Image Bank (p. 24) Courtesy of
　　　NASA/JPL (p. 40-47) Pluto-Courtesy
　　　of U.S. Naval Observatory (p. 46)
　　　Courtesy of Royal Observatory
　　　Edinburgh (p. 47).

Time-Life Books Inc. is a wholly owned subsidiary of THE TIME INC. BOOK COMPANY.

TIME-LIFE is a trademark of Time Warner Inc. U.S.A.

FISHER-PRICE, LITTLE PEOPLE and AWNING DESIGN are trademarks of Fisher-Price, Division of The Quaker Oats Company, and are used under license.

Time-Life Books Inc. offers a wide range of fine publications, including home video products. For subscription information, call 1-800-621-7026, or write TIME-LIFE BOOKS, P.O. Box C-32068, Richmond, Virginia 23261-2068.

ACKNOWLEDGMENTS

Every effort has been made to trace the ownership of all copyrighted material and to secure the necessary permissions to reprint these selections. If any question arises as to the use of any material, the editor and the publisher, while expressing regret for any inadvertent error, will make the necessary correction in future printings.

Grateful acknowledgment is made to the following for permission to reprint copyrighted material: Crown Publishers Inc. for BEYOND THE MILKY WAY by Cecile Schoberle. Copyright © 1986 by Cecile Schoberle. Margaret Hillert for "Farther Than Far" and "Space Swing." International Creative Management for British rights for TO SPACE AND BACK by Sally Ride and Susan Okie. Copyright © 1986 by Sally Ride and Susan Okie. Lothrop, Lee & Shepard Books (a div. of William Morrow & Co.) for US and Canadian rights for TO SPACE AND BACK by Sally Ride and Susan Okie. Copyright © 1986 by Sally Ride and Susan Okie. William Morrow & Co. for "Naughty Little Brown Mouse" from RIDE A PURPLE PELICAN by Jack Prelutsky. Copyright © 1986 by Jack Prelutsky. Marian Reiner for "Secrets" from SPACE SONGS by Myra Cohn Livingston. Copyright © 1988 by Myra Cohn Livingston. Published by Holiday House, New York.

TIME-LIFE BOOKS
ALEXANDRIA, VIRGINIA

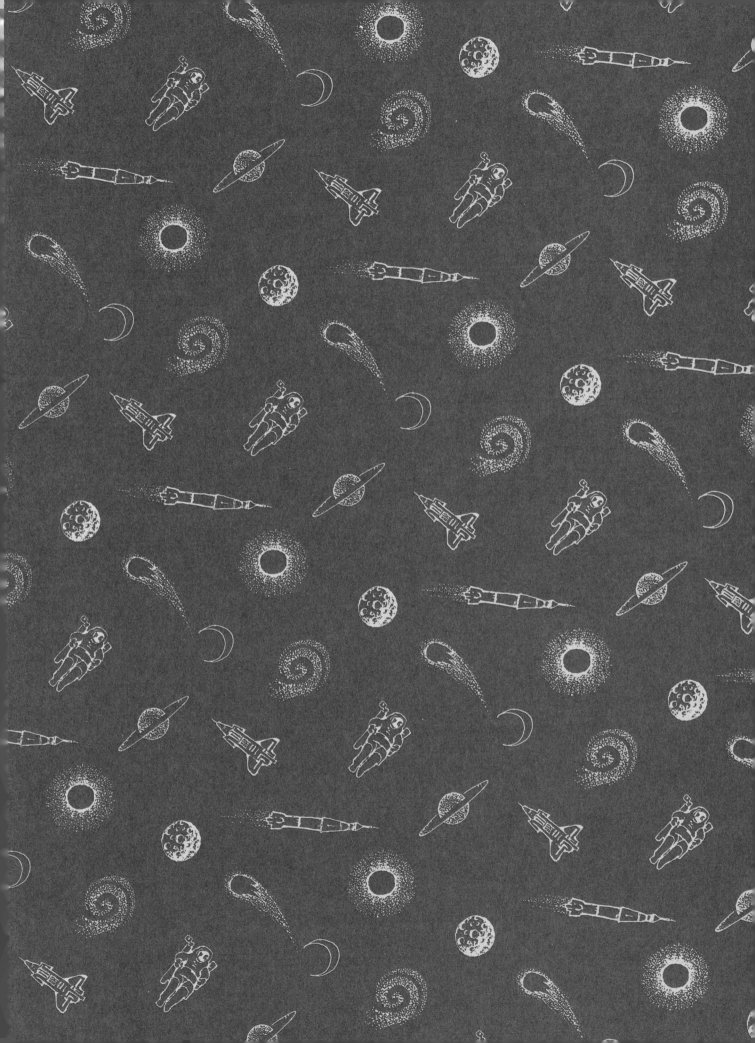

Secrets

Space keeps its secrets
                    hidden.
It does not tell.

          Are black holes time machines?
          Where do lost comets go?

          Is Pluto moon or planet?

How many, how vast
     unknown galaxies beyond us?

     Do other creatures
     dwell   on distant spheres?

                    Will we ever know?

Space is silent.
It seldom answers.

     But we ask.

Myra Cohn Livingston